THIS JOURNAL BELONGS TO :

"Anything worth having is worth waiting for."

Made in the USA
Monee, IL
18 December 2021

86356573R00070